AMERICA'S SECRET WEAPON

AMERICA'S SECRET WEAPON

Navajo Code Talkers of World War II

ANN STALCUP

Sunstone
Press

SANTA FE

Sunstone books may be purchased for educational, business, or sales promotional use.
For information please write: Special Markets Department, Sunstone Press,
P.O. Box 2321, Santa Fe, New Mexico 87504-2321.
Book and Cover design by Vicki Ahl
Body typeface › ITC Benguiat Std
Printed on acid-free paper
∞

Library of Congress Cataloging-in-Publication Data

Names: Stalcup, Ann, 1935- author.
Title: America's secret weapon : Navajo code talkers of World War II / by Ann
    Stalcup.
Other titles: Navajo code talkers of World War II
Description: Santa Fe : Sunstone Press, [2017]
Identifiers: LCCN 2017003419 | ISBN 9781632931764 (softcover : alk. paper)
Subjects: LCSH: Navajo code talkers–Juvenile literature. | Navajo
    Indians–History–20th century–Juvenile literature. | Navajo
    language–History–20th century–Juvenile literature. | World War,
    1939-1945–Cryptography–Juvenile literature. | World War,
    1939-1945–Participation, Indian–Juvenile literature.
Classification: LCC D810.C88 S74 2017 | DDC 940.54/8673–dc23
LC record available at https://lccn.loc.gov/2017003419

SUNSTONE PRESS IS COMMITTED TO MINIMIZING OUR ENVIRONMENTAL IMPACT ON THE PLANET. THE PAPER USED IN THIS BOOK IS
FROM RESPONSIBLY MANAGED FORESTS. OUR PRINTER HAS RECEIVED CHAIN OF CUSTODY (COC) CERTIFICATION FROM: THE FOREST
STEWARDSHIP COUNCIL™ (FSC®), PROGRAMME FOR THE ENDORSEMENT OF FOREST CERTIFICATION™ (PEFC™), AND THE SUSTAINABLE
FORESTRY INITIATIVE® (SFI®). THE FSC® COUNCIL IS A NON-PROFIT ORGANIZATION, PROMOTING THE ENVIRONMENTALLY
APPROPRIATE, SOCIALLY BENEFICIAL AND ECONOMICALLY VIABLE MANAGEMENT OF THE WORLD'S FORESTS. FSC® CERTIFICATION IS
RECOGNIZED INTERNATIONALLY AS A RIGOROUS ENVIRONMENTAL AND SOCIAL STANDARD FOR RESPONSIBLE FOREST MANAGEMENT.

WWW.SUNSTONEPRESS.COM
SUNSTONE PRESS / POST OFFICE BOX 2321 / SANTA FE, NM 87504-2321 /USA
(505) 988-4418 / ORDERS ONLY (800) 243-5644 / FAX (505) 988-1025

This book is dedicated to four brave Navajo men who generously shared their stories with me: Wilfred Billey, Keith Little, and Albert Smith, and especially to Chester Nez. For the most part, this is his story.

Foreword

The Navajo reservation where the boys in this story spent their childhood covers 25,000 square miles. The "res" as it is often called, lies mostly in Arizona but also spreads into New Mexico, Utah, and Colorado.

The Navajo is the largest of the Native American groups. Since they are geographically isolated from other tribes, the Navajo speak a common language that has remained pure throughout the centuries. It is also mostly unwritten.

Few people other than Navajo are fluent in the language, and, until Navajo boys were forced to attend boarding schools, most Navajo could not speak English. Through the inspiration of one man, the Navajo language played a vital role in helping America win the war against the Japanese in the Pacific during World War II. Although all of the facts are true, this fictionalized story is one account of the Navajo Code Talkers, America's Secret Weapon.

Prologue

Sam found it impossible to get used to the sound of gunfire hour after hour, or to ignore the soldiers who were hit by bullets. Bombs exploded all around them, the air thick with smoke.

Everyone seemed to be yelling at once. Bodies lay everywhere and the young Navajo men had difficulty ignoring them. Everything was so different from their peaceful home lives. Wounded soldiers screamed for help but no one came to their aid. As a young boy, Sam had no idea that this horrifying scene would later be part of his future.

1

Life On The Reservation

"They cut off your hair," Sam's friend Joe told him. "And they wash your mouth out with soap when you speak Navajo."

"Who told you that?" asked Sam.

"My brother. He started boarding school last year."

"Why?" asked Sam.

"My brother said they don't want us to be Navajo. We must look and talk like other American boys."

"But I don't speak English," said Sam. "If that is what's going to happen to me, I'm never going to school."

Often, Sam and his herd of sheep and goats wandered to where a friend watched his own family's herd. Joe's brother attended a government boarding school and Sam did not like what he'd just heard. But Sam had no choice. He was almost six. Sooner or later he, too, would be forced to leave his home on the reservation and go to school. It was the law. And if his friend was right, his long black hair would soon be gone.

"Your hair is part of your homeland," his parents often said. "It must never be cut. To lose one's hair is to lose one's ability to think. It is the Navajo way to have long hair."

Until that moment, Sam's childhood had been much like that of many other young Navajo boys. Few roads crossed the huge Navajo reservation and Sam and his family lived peaceful, simple lives, isolated from towns and cities. Their possessions were few and so were their needs.

As a small boy, Sam learned to adapt to the extreme heat and severe cold. Day after day, as the sheep and goats wandered along nibbling at the sparse, dry grass, Sam had lots of time to think and dream and draw. Sam drew the people, plants, and animals he saw each day. With his sketch pad and pencil he tried to capture the glorious sunsets, the leaping deer, and the shadows of the clouds as they crossed the vast empty land. Each day was much like the next. Days were long. Sketching helped Sam pass the time. Imagining leaving his beloved land filled Sam with a deep sadness.

2

Boarding School

As the hot, dry summer drew to a close, six-year-old Sam knew that soon he would have to leave. A few days earlier, a man from the boarding school had visited his parents. He informed them that their son must be ready to leave in three days. But his parents did not tell Sam. They knew he dreaded leaving the reservation and how scared he was. He could take nothing with him. The school provided their students with everything they needed including coveralls to wear.

Late one afternoon, as Sam returned to the hogan tired and hungry, he heard the unmistakable sound of an approaching truck. A knot formed in Sam's stomach. "Is this the day?" he wondered. A cloud of dust rose behind the truck as it bounced across the rough ground. As the vehicle came closer, Sam saw that one man rode in the cab. Several boys sat in the truck's bed.

"Time to go!" said the driver. "I haven't got all day." After hugging his parents, Sam reluctantly climbed aboard. "Take this fry bread," his mother said. "I made it especially for you this morning. You will be hungry on the journey." With shaking hands, Sam stuffed the fry bread into his small cloth sack, his sketch pad and pencil already hidden inside.

The truck driver stopped three times before reaching the government school in Fort Defiance, New Mexico. Sam's friend Joe climbed on last. He and Sam were both starting school for the first time. The other boys chattered away, happy to see each other after the long summer break, but Sam and Joe were silent. And, as the truck took Sam further and further away from home, he thought his heart would break.

Within hours Sam's worst nightmares came true. A man hacked off his long black hair. "Am I still a Navajo?" Sam wondered as he looked at his jet black hair lying on the floor.

Sam attended the school in Fort Defiance for eight long years. The days crept by. Whenever Sam worked too slowly, or spoke Navajo, they washed his mouth out with bitter-tasting lye soap. "Will my time here ever end?" he wondered.

School seemed like a prison. Sam hated the strict rules. He missed his family. He longed for his family. He missed caring for the sheep and goats. No longer could he enjoy carefree days on the reservation. Each year, as time crawled by, Sam thought vacation time would never come. In June he could escape the school and its strict rules. He could once again enjoy time in his peaceful home with his loving family.

Each summer, a truck took Sam and Joe back to the reservation. Often, when it disposed of its cargo, the boys were forced to walk the last five or ten miles in the scorching heat. Perhaps the driver couldn't wait to be free of the boys just as they couldn't wait to be free of the school.

As each summer drew to a close, Sam was once again filled with dread. But although Sam hated school, he formed friendships, learned to speak English, do arithmetic, and studied science and history. But the only time Sam felt truly at peace was when he took out his sketch pad. Always he drew scenes of home, the animals, the scenery, the sunsets, the desert plants, and the faces of his family. In his mind he saw them as clearly as if he were still on the reservation.

3

Sam's High School Years

As a teenager, Sam attended schools in Gallup, New Mexico, and then Tuba City, Arizona. Sometimes, he and his friend Roy talked about the experiences they had had at their previous schools.

"I'll never forget the terrible day when they cut off my hair and the faces of my parents as they first saw me," Sam told Roy. "I felt as if I were no longer Navajo." Roy was lucky. He hadn't had that experience. At the schools Roy attended, the instructors were kind to the boys. They seemed to understand the difficult adjustment the boys made when they left their homes on the reservation to attend boarding school.

Sam enjoyed high school more than his years in Fort Defiance, but he still missed life on the reservation. At night, he lay in bed thinking about his homeland. He missed his family and his peaceful life as a sheepherder. He missed the huge empty spaces, the sweetness of the bird calls, the beauty of the deer as they leaped, and, after dark, the howl of coyotes and the hoot of owls. The terrible ache inside him never seemed to go away.

Even when Sam found time to draw, he never felt at peace in the crowded boarding school. Sometimes his drawings brought the people and creatures that he loved closer; on other occasions, his sketches made him feel more homesick than ever. The other boys never seemed to stop talking. "I hate it here," he often said to his friend Roy. "I wish I could leave."

On December 7, 1941, as Sam and Roy lay on their beds talking quietly and listening to music on the radio, a voice said, "We interrupt this program to bring you a special news bulletin. The Japanese have attacked Pearl Harbor, Hawaii."

When they heard the news, Sam felt powerless, trapped, a prisoner. He wanted to help America fight the Japanese. "What can I do?" he wondered. He already knew that in Europe World War II had been raging since 1939, but so far, America was not involved.

Sam and the other Navajo often spoke with bitterness of the "Long Walk," the time in 1864 when the White Man forced almost 9,000 Navajo to leave their lands and walk the 300 miles to Fort Sumner, New Mexico like a herd of sheep. But in spite of that, the Navajo were still loyal Americans.

"If I were a soldier, I could defend my homeland," Sam thought.

Sam and Roy were restless and anxious.

"There must be some way to leave school and join the fight," said Sam.

But it didn't seem possible. The boys didn't know that in California one man worked on a plan where their skills as Navajo would play an important role in fighting the war in the Pacific and change their lives forever.

4

An Ingenious Plan

Philip Johnston, a white man, grew up on the Navajo reservation. His father was a missionary and both Philip and his father spoke Navajo fluently. As a soldier in Europe during World War I, Johnston had learned the importance of codes during wartime.

At the time of the Pearl Harbor bombing, Johnston was considered too old to join the armed services. In early 1942, determined to help the war effort in some way, he contacted the Naval Office in Los Angeles. "I believe the Navajo language could be used as a code," he told them.

Sent to Camp Elliot near San Diego, Johnson met with Major James E. Jones. When the major heard Johnston speaking Navajo, he was convinced. "What strange sounds!" he thought. "This could work," Major Jones told the other officers. "Since Navajo is a mostly unwritten language, it would be extremely difficult to decode."

Philip Johnston next organized a demonstration. Four young Navajo men were brought to the San Diego naval base and Johnson told them,

"We'd like you to pass these messages back and forth," he said. "You are to write down their translations in English."

With Major Jones and General Clayton B. Vogel as witnesses, the demonstration began. "Look at this!" exclaimed General Vogel. "The messages have been translated perfectly." Philip Johnson felt overjoyed. His experiment had been successful.

Now the plan had to be put into action. Two hundred Navajo

boys would be enlisted. Having learned English at boarding schools, many had trained in various trades. They had the skills needed for developing a Navajo code, for translating messages from Navajo into English, and working as radio men.

"Their assignment is to pass messages back and forth from the front lines to base camp during invasions," said Major Jones. "Their assistance in tracking troop movements will be invaluable, particularly if the Japanese are unable to decipher their code."

5

A Chance to Escape

May 4th, 1942, was a day Sam never forgot. Three uniformed Marine Corps recruiters visited his boarding school in Tuba City. The boys gathered in the school meeting hall. Three Marines stood at attention on the stage. To the boys, the marines looked magnificent in their smart uniforms.

"What do they want?" Sam whispered. "Why are they here?"

Gradually the whispering stopped. The audience was silent, expectant, waiting. Each boy held his breath. Then one of the Marines spoke. "We need volunteers for a special assignment," he said. "Boys seventeen years or older. They must speak both Navajo and English fluently."

Sam needed no time to think about it. He hated school and he hated the Japanese for attacking America. He wanted to help win the war. He turned to his friend, Roy, and said, "Let's get out of here!" Roy didn't need any persuading.

"This school is like a prison," said Sam. "Here's our chance to leave." Many other boys were anxious to escape. Some volunteers were only fourteen, but the reservation keeps no birth records. No one knew the true age of the volunteers. Sam was only fifteen and Roy was sixteen.

Needing his parents' permission before he could enlist, Sam returned to the reservation. His parents, like many other Navajo adults, had never learned to read. Sam knew that if he explained the reason for the documents, they would refuse to sign them. And so, like other parents unable to read or write, Sam's parents used thumb prints to sign the permission forms. It wasn't until Sam and Roy completed boot camp that their families learned the truth. It was too late for them to withdraw their permission. The boys were going to war.

Although between 200 and 300 Navajo boys volunteered for the training, the planned task had not yet been tested on the battlefront. And since it was untested, funds were approved for only 30 boys. Sam and Roy were selected. They possessed all of the qualifications needed for the job ahead of them. Fluent in English, they were intelligent, and had been trained to work with many kinds of machinery.

Those not chosen for the special training joined the Army, Navy, or Air Force. None of them planned to return to boarding school. This was their chance for a new and exciting life. By the end of the war, 450 young Navajo boys had been recruited. Only thirty failed to complete the course.

"What is expected of us?" Sam and Roy often wondered, but to them, anything was better than boarding school. They had no idea that in a few short months their lives would change completely. Their ability to speak both English and Navajo fluently made them one of the most valuable weapons the United States had in fighting the war in the Pacific. No longer would they be punished for using their native tongue.

6

Boot Camp

On May 6, 1942, just two days after they'd volunteered, Sam and the other boys began their long bus journey to San Diego. Only 29 of the 30 boys who were selected had shown up. Some were nervous; others, like Sam and Roy, were excited.

"What's going to happen to us?" said one.

"What do you think they want us to do?" said another.

"Will we be going to Japan?" asked a third boy. "Are we going to fight the enemy?"

Sam and Roy were too excited to talk. They sat silently, their minds spinning as they each thought about what the future might bring.

Sam and Roy had never been in a city as large as San Diego and neither of them had ever seen the ocean. Their eyes darted everywhere, but the bus whisked them along. All too soon they entered the Marine Base, their home for the next two months.

For most Marines, the two months of boot camp is the hardest part of their training. Days are long. And for those unused to running or walking long distances, each day is torture. But it seemed to the other Marines that nothing seemed to bother the young Navajo boys. They took everything in stride.

On the Navajo reservation, homes are small and every family member is expected to keep his things neat and orderly. The Marines expect the same out of their boys. Every day, uniforms are freshly cleaned and pressed. The neatness of the bunks and equipment is of utmost importance. On the reservation, cooperation between family members and tribe members is also expected. Life in the Marines is the same. Each man is part of a team, a "clan." In battle, survival depends on teamwork.

"We'll show them what we're made of," said Sam.

Sam and Roy and their Navajo companions quickly proved they could handle anything they were asked to do. The men in charge of their training had never seen anything like it. They didn't realize that from an early age, Navajo children quickly learn to adapt to the extreme heat and severe cold that is part of their everyday lives. They are used to long walks in intense heat with little food and water. Their harsh upbringings made it easy for the boys to adapt to the hardships of boot camp and to excel at every challenge they were given.

"This is nothing!" said Sam.

7

The Task

When boot camp ended, the boys moved to nearby Camp Elliot. They felt nervous as they were led into a classroom and told to sit down. None of the boys was anxious to start school again, and this looked like school to them. But moments later Sam, Roy, and their companions finally learned what their task would be.

"We need you to create a code," said their instructor. "You must find a Navajo word to represent each letter of the alphabet. Later you will find words for items that are important in fighting a war. Using your code, you will be responsible for sending messages between groups of American troops fighting in the Pacific. If the Japanese are unable to break the code, the code will help America defeat the Japanese."

With those words the instructor left the room, locking the door behind him as he went.

The boys fell silent. Then Sam could control himself no longer.

"I can't believe it!" he said. "Our whole lives white men have punished us for speaking Navajo; now they want us because we speak Navajo!"

Sam and Roy and the other boys were excited about the challenge. They took their assignment seriously. Letter by letter, the boys chose a Navajo word for each letter of the alphabet. To make remembering them easy, they chose words important in the Navajo culture.

"For 'a', we can use 'wol-la-chee,' ant in English?" said one boy.

"And how about 'na-hash-chid,' badger, for "b," said another boy.

"C" should be '*moasi*,' cat," said Sam.

Each evening, the code was locked in a safe and the boys were reminded of the secrecy of their task. No one must know what they were working on or the code would be abandoned.

The group had no teacher and no leader. No one argued about the choices they made. The Navajo way is to make decisions peacefully. The boys worked efficiently and quickly.

The alphabet completed, the next step was to find a word for items such as guns, bombs, tanks, jeeps, and different types of planes and ships. But that wasn't all. Marine divisions, the ranks of officers, and countries all had to be assigned code words.

The boys were unfamiliar with many of the things they had to name. They didn't know what the planes and ships and other pieces of equipment looked like or how they were used. Although there were no words in the Navajo language for these things, it was necessary for the boys to choose words meaningful to them or they would be unable to remember them. To solve this problem, the instructor provided the boys with pictures of the items they were to name. He explained the characteristics of each so that they could find the most appropriate word.

Different types of planes were named for the jobs they did and the birds the boys were most familiar with. A dive bomber became a *gini*, a chicken hawk, an observation plane was an owl, *ne-as-jah*, a fighter plane reminded them of a hummingbird, *da-he-tih-hi*. Ships were also named to match their shape or the jobs they did. A battleship looked like a whale, *lo-tso*; an aircraft carrier became a bird carrier, *tsidi-moffa-ye-hi*; and a destroyer was a shark, *ca-lo*. In all, the completed code contained 211 words.

Later on in the war, it became necessary to add other words for many of the letters used in the code. Enemy code breakers listen for letters or words that are repeated frequently since they usually represent letters like "a," "i," "e" or words like "the" or "and." No one must be able to translate or break the Navajo code.

Until then, every code ever developed in military history had been broken, so the boys faced quite a challenge. As the war progressed, equipment changed and new equipment was added, even more words were needed. The final code consisted of 411 words.

8

Learning to Survive

The days continued to be long for Sam and the other boys. When their hours in the classroom ended, the boys spent their evenings studying the organization of the military. The boys also learned to take weapons apart, clean, and reassemble them. Learning how to defend themselves was essential. Some days Sam thought his head would burst with the information he need to understand and memorize. But he never complained.

Once the code was completed, the most important phase of the boys' training began: learning how to send and receive messages swiftly and accurately. Incoming messages would begin with the word "Talker." Messages about troop positions and casualties would be transmitted from the Navajo "talker" on the front lines to the Navajo receiver in the rear. The receiver had to translate the incoming coded message in his head, then write the message down accurately in English and deliver the translated message to the nearest command post. If a radio failed, the "talkers" quickly repaired it themselves.

The talkers also learned to send and receive messages in Morse Code. From time to time the use of Morse code might be necessary. Once the talkers reached the Pacific islands where the battles were being fought, a lot would depend on them doing their job well. They had a vital role to play if America was to be victorious in fighting the Japanese.

Sam and the other boys needed to learn to defend themselves in combat, but they also needed survival skills. Operating a radio and sending the code successfully was only one of the many skills they needed. Both day and night, for hours at a time, the boys were sent out in pairs. Heavy radio transmitters were carried in backpacks. One boy cranked the radio while his partner sent a message. In another location, two other Navajo boys received the message and translated it. The boys were quickly becoming men and were even referred to as "radio men."

For Sam, one of his worst experiences occurred 30 miles out at sea. Wearing their heavy radio equipment, the boys were ordered to jump off a ship and into the water far below. Although they had life jackets, they felt terrified. Sam and Roy were two of the lucky ones. As young children, they had learned how to swim in a pond on the reservation, but since the radios weighed around 80 to 90 pounds each, they thought the weight of the radios would surely cause them all to drown. But once again, every Navajo boy passed the test with flying colors.

Their training finally ended. Each boy had committed the code to memory. Each boy knew how to care for his weapon and how to survive in all kinds of circumstances. The boys had also learned how to use and repair their radios. It was time for active duty.

A copy of the code would not travel with the boys. They must rely on their memories. But that was no problem for them. Life on the reservation had trained them to retain information and relay messages. That and their powers of observation were part of the Navajo culture, dating back to the days when few, if any, Navajo could read or write.

"Will I ever return?" Sam wondered as he looked back across the huge ocean. It was something he would wonder about often as the days and months and years passed and the fighting continued. Already his home and family seemed very far away.

Twenty-seven of the twenty-nine Navajo Radio Men crossed the Pacific. Two-hundred more Navajo boys had already completed boot camp and two of the original group of twenty-nine boys remained behind to teach the code to the new recruits. The military leaders felt convinced that the code would be successful and were recruiting even more Navajo. In the end, 450 young Navajo boys were trained to work as code talkers.

9

In the Thick of the Fighting

When their ship reached the island of Guadalcanal, a short distance northeast of Australia, Sam, his friend Roy, and the other Navajo Marines waded ashore, their heavy radio equipment on their backs. Dead bodies floated in the water and lay around them on the ground. Sam and Roy were in the thick of battle.

Immediately, pairs of Navajo were sent to the front lines. Their job was to relay messages in Navajo to the Navajo teams at the command post some distance away. People were depending on the ability of the "talkers" to send messages quickly. The Navajo "receivers" had to translate them accurately in order to keep the soldiers on the front lines safe. A mistake in translation could cause the deaths of numerous soldiers. It was a huge responsibility.

"Will the code work?" Sam wondered. "Will I let my companions down?"

Although Sam and the other Navajo "talkers" were young, their companions teased them and called them "Chief" after the many Indian chiefs they'd seen in movies. But the white men, or *belegaana* as the Navajo called them, also showed respect for the important job the Navajo were doing as radio men. They had no idea the messages were being sent in a Navajo code.

Sam and Roy were assigned to the front lines where the battle raged fiercely. With speed the boys relayed messages about troop and enemy positions. At the rear, the men receiving and decoding each message delivered them quickly and accurately to the command post.

The Navajo boys worked as a team, trusting each other to do their job well. It was the only way to survive. The "talkers" were jubilant. The code was a success.

Sam found it difficult to get used to the sound of gunfire hour after hour or to ignore the soldiers who were hit by bullets. Bombs exploded all around them and the air was thick with smoke. Everyone seemed to be yelling at once. Bodies lay everywhere and it was difficult for the Navajo radio men to ignore them. Wounded soldiers screamed for help, but no one seemed available to help them.

The Navajo have a great fear of "chindi," spirits, the ghosts of the dead, believing that only the evil part of a person remains on earth after someone dies. Because of these spirits, no Navajo should ever step over a dead body but scared as they were, they learned to adjust to the circumstances. Sam told Roy, "We have a job to do. We must do it well."

Island by island they battled on—Bouganville, Guam, and Peleliu. Sam and Roy were attached to the 1st and then 3rd Marine Divisions. Island by island Sam and the other "talkers" played their part in defeating the Japanese. Steadily they moved north across the Pacific Ocean where one battle after another was fought and won. Many men were killed but the Japanese were pushed farther and farther back toward their homeland.

The men fought in the most miserable conditions imaginable. Some areas receive up to 200 inches of rain a year. But together, belegaana, white men, and Navajo alike pushed their way through muddy, insect-infested jungles, up rocky slopes, across swamps and deep bogs, each man carrying at least 100 pounds of equipment on his back.

Booby traps rigged by the enemy presented another danger. The insects were unbearable. Mosquitos and leeches were everywhere. And there were crocodiles and numerous snakes. The Navajo boys had been taught never to kill snakes, so it must have been hard for them to watch their companions killing any snake that lay across their path. "Snakes are God's creatures," Sam often said.

"They have a job to do on this earth, just as we do."

Many Navajo carried buckskin pouches with them. The pouches contained corn pollen which the boys believed protected them. Others carried small bags of medicine made from the gallbladders of creatures such as skunks and mountain lions. These provided protection to Navajo who traveled among strangers. Some Navajos prayed to the spirits for protection before sending and receiving messages.

Even in battle, the Navajo boys repeatedly demonstrated their ability to withstand any hardships. They had no difficulty going without food for several days. They had experienced many challenges in their lives and their Navajo upbringing had prepared them for anything the war in the Pacific could throw at them.

The Japanese had a reputation for bravery and daring. They were masters at hiding themselves and surprising the enemy, but the Navajo were much better. Not all Navajo were radio men. Those who were part of the regular armed services were experts at tracking. They moved soundlessly, were equally comfortable in daylight and in darkness, and excelled at close combat.

In the assault on each new island, marine "talkers" were usually at the front, the "first wave" as it was called. Command centers had to be set up immediately so that enemy positions could be radioed to the troops. This strategy saved many lives but it also put the "talkers" in great danger. Often Sam and Roy were assigned to the front lines. On other occasions they were based in the battalion headquarters. Most often they crawled through mud or dense jungle on their bellies. But no matter where they were, or how much danger they were in, they relayed and translated messages calmly, skillfully, and accurately. As close friends, their teamwork was superb. By doing their job well, each Navajo team saved thousands of lives. The American troops always knew exactly where the Japanese were hiding and the Japanese never knew what made the American soldiers so successful.

10

A Close Call

The Japanese had their own radio men. They also had code breakers who were among the most successful code breakers in the world. There had never been a code they couldn't decipher. But what the Japanese code breakers suddenly heard over the American airwaves didn't match any code they'd ever heard before. They were completely baffled. And although they spent long hours trying, it was impossible to decipher the strange sounds. The Navajo code remained unbroken.

Both the Japanese and the Navajo had dark skin and black hair. Occasionally, when Navajo "talkers" ventured behind enemy lines to spy on the Japanese, they blended in without anyone realizing who they were. But it was a dangerous thing to do. And because they looked like the Japanese, some Navajo boys almost became victims of American bullets in what is called "friendly fire." They had a hard time talking their way out of some dangerous situations they found themselves in.

On Peleliu Sam and Roy were sent to work with the 144th Army Division. One day, as they returned to the base, their own men mistook them for Japanese. "Halt!" a voice yelled. "Halt or I'll shoot!" As one soldier held a 45 caliber handgun to Sam's head, his partner held a rifle on Roy.

Although Sam was frightened, he tried to stay calm. "Contact the tank we're communicating with," he told the soldiers. "They will tell you who we are." The officer in the tank responded immediately.

"They are American radio men," he said. "Let them go!" And the danger passed.

In order to avoid putting the boys in that situation again, it was decided that a non-Navajo, a *belegaana*, must accompany the Navajo radio men at all times. It wasn't until the war ended that Sam and the other "talkers" learned that they'd had a bodyguard for much of the time they'd been in the combat zone.

There was rarely any peace from the fighting, but whenever there were a few moments of quiet, out would come Sam's sketch book. Drawing gave Sam a sense of peace, and sketching the animals, plants, and people he loved made home seem much closer.

"Will I ever see my family?" Sam often wondered. "Will I ever again enjoy the peace and solitude of the reservation?" Occasionally he allowed himself to dream, but most of the time he was too busy to think of himself. He thought only of the lives he could save if he did his job well.

The boys who fought in the Pacific were always in the minds of their families on the reservation. Although they had no idea of the specific job their boys were doing, they knew that they must be in constant danger. Often, prayer feathers were placed in the ground to protect the boys. In May 1944, the families of 150 of the boys gathered on the reservation to hold an Enemy Way ceremony. Photographs of the boys were placed on the ground in front of the singer. Like many Navajo ceremonies, the Enemy Way ceremony continued for many hours.

The skills developed by the Navajo on the reservation continued to assist them. They ignored the many hardships they experienced, and the tracking and scouting skills developed as children proved invaluable during jungle combat. As Navajo, they had a centuries-old history of sending and receiving messages accurately, although using drums or smoke signals to send messages was rather different from the radio work they were doing now.

The Americans troops fought on, day after day, month after month, year after year. Sometimes Sam and Roy relayed messages to and from a Navy ship anchored close to the shore; at other times they were on the front lines, in the heart of battle, always focused on the job they needed to do, much too busy to be scared.

As the American Army, Navy, and Air Force fought their way across the Pacific islands, the Radio Men continued to play their part in the success of each battle. Although 21,000 Americans were lost in the battle of Iwo Jima, the American troops finally captured the island in March, 1945. The Japanese fought as fiercely as ever but the Americans continued to drive them northward towards their home land. The end of the war might be in sight.

Japan surrendered on September 2, 1945, four months after the war ended in Europe. In all, thirteen "talkers" were killed in battle. Three of them were from the original twenty-nine. The Navajo code was the only unbreakable code ever developed by any country for use during a war. Perhaps it would be needed again. And so each code talker was told, "The Navajo code has been classified as 'Top Secret.' You can tell no one, not even your family, about the code you created. It is vital that the code remains a secret. Some day we may need to use it again."

11

Time to Go Home

Sam and Roy returned to San Diego to be discharged. As the troop ship slid silently into the harbor so many images flashed through Sam's mind. It had been three years since he had left, but it felt like a lifetime. He couldn't imagine he'd only been fifteen years old, a boy, when he was last there. He had experienced things no man should ever have to see. At eighteen years old, he was a man.

Sam felt lost. No longer a schoolboy, he had no idea what to do with the rest of his life. Should he return to the reservation or stay in California for a while as many of his buddies planned to do? His friend, Roy, had already left for the reservation.

Sam knew his family was anxious to see him, but he wasn't ready to go home just yet. He had seen and survived so much killing and destruction. He needed to forget all of the horrors he'd experienced.

One by one the boys returned home. In their absence, blessing ceremonies had been held in hopes of keeping the boys safe. When Sam finally arrived on the reservation, there was great rejoicing. A medicine man came to his family's home and a Squaw Dance was held. Sam's body had to be cleansed of the evil he had seen.

Once the ceremonies were over, each day seemed just as it had been when he left. His family was delighted that for the time being he planned to remain at home. Unsure about his future, Sam once again cared for his family's herd of sheep and goats. But instead of the feeling of peace he expected to find, the horrors of the war still crowded his mind and his senses.

Month after month, each bird call sounded to Sam like the scream of someone hit by mortar fire. The sudden movement of a leaping deer startled him. The woodpeckers reminded him of the staccato sound of gunfire. At the hiss of a snake, Sam was once again fighting his way through the snake-ridden jungles. Even in the gathering darkness, images of war filled Sam's mind. Each hoot of an owl reminded him of the signal he and his Navajo companions used to verify each other's positions. And when he picked up his pencil and sketch pad, instead of the people and animals he had always drawn, other images crowed his mind and drawing was impossible.

"Will I ever find peace?" Sam wondered. "If only I could talk to my family or friends about how I feel. Perhaps then I could find a way to live with the horrors I have seen." He could speak to no one about the code, but he found it impossible to talk about anything he had seen or experienced. His family honored his silence and asked no questions.

Sam cared for his family's sheep and goats for three years, but one day, when he picked up his sketch pad and pencil, he found himself once again drawing the people, animals, and plants that he loved. He was finally at peace. Those three years had given him time to think. And plan. And draw.

Time Line

1941 to Present Day

1941–1945: The war against Germany is fought on the continent of Europe and in North Africa. In the Pacific, as Admiral Nimitz describes it, the battle ground is quite different. American troops have to win the war against Japan by "island hopping," which means capturing the Pacific island by island as they move north through the Pacific islands towards Japan. During 1941 and 1942, fighting rages on Guadalcanal, the first island that has to be captured. Once the Japanese on Guadalcanal have been defeated, and the island belongs to the Americans, it becomes home base for a great many servicemen. After each battle, the troops return to Guadalcanal by troop ship or transport plane for what is known as "R and R"—rest and recreation.

1945: World War II against Japan ends on September 2. The Code Talkers' role in the war remains a secret. Many Navajo who fought in the war are persuaded by their former teachers to return to school. Some earn their high school diplomas. The Government's G.I. Bill pays the tuition for those who want to attend college.

1968: Twenty-three years after the war ends, the "talkers" are flown to Chicago by Air Force jet. Their families, who travel to Chicago by train, have no knowledge of the role their husbands, fathers, brothers, and sons played in the fight against Japan. The secret had remained a secret. The men are honored in a special ceremony. Many of them have not seen each other since the war. The "talkers" are now free to discuss their role as radio men. Gradually, through books and newspapers, America and their families learn of the contribution the Navajo Code Talkers made to winning the war in the Pacific. The Navajo Code is recognized as the only unbroken code in military history.

1971: A Navajo Code Talkers Association is founded in Window Rock, Arizona. Each part of the newly created uniform stands for something meaningful in the Navajo culture: the red hat represents the U.S. Marine Corps, the gold jacket represents corn pollen, the beige pants are the color of Mother Earth, and the black shoes represent the four sacred mountains of Navajoland. The turquoise and silver necklace worn around each talkers' neck is a symbol of the Navajo people since turquoise, plentiful in the area, is always worn on ceremonial occasions. Once a month the Code Talkers meet at the Chamber of Commerce building in Gallup, New Mexico. The walls of the meeting house are lined with Code Talker memorabilia—medals, uniforms, documents, and photographs.

1982: Thirty-seven years after World War II ends, the Code Talkers finally receive public recognition for their bravery. President Ronald Reagan declares August 14 National Code Talkers' Day.

1992: A Code Talker is selected to send a prayer for peace from Phoenix, Arizona to the government Press Room in Washington, DC. Keith Little, a member of the first group of Code Talkers, is there to receive the message. He translates the message perfectly. Fifty years after its creation, the code passes the test once again.

2001: On July 26, in Washington DC, President Bush presents four Code Talkers from the original twenty-nine with the Congressional Gold Medal. Only one other survivor is still alive. He is too ill to attend the ceremony. President Bush speaks of the Code Talkers' success in relaying messages and in doing so, saving thousands of lives and helping to win World War II. The medal depicts two Code Talkers operating a radio. It is a proud moment for the four men.

2001: In November, in Window Rock, Arizona, four hundred men receive a Congressional Silver Medal. These men are survivors from the Navajo groups that trained after the creation of the code. Chester Nez is one of more than 3,000 people who gather there to witness this historic event. The medal is surrounded by turquoise beads and bears a picture of Ira Hayes, the Pima Indian who helped raise the U.S. flag over Mount Surabachi on the island of Iwo Jima. It honors not only the brave Code Talkers but also commemorates the battle for control of Iwo Jima, one of the bloodiest and hardest fought battles in the war to control the Pacific. The talkers start traveling all over the country talking with adults and children about their unbreakable code. They are treated as heroes.

In 1950, the U.S. is involved in a war against North Korea. After spending three years at home on the reservation, Chester is forced to rejoin the Marines. Fortunately he spends two years in Hawaii and does not have to fight.

In 1953, the Korean War ends. Chester earns his high school diploma and begins work as a house painter. He continues to sketch in his spare time. When he settles in Albuquerque, New Mexico, he paints a mural on one of the buildings.

At age 27, Chester marries; he has four children and one adopted son. Chester became grandfather to twelve grandchildren and lived with one of his sons in Albuquerque, New Mexico. He had a peaceful life, quite different from the almost four years he spent as a Code Talker.

Receiving the Congressional Gold Medal in 2001 from President Bush was Chester's proudest moment.

Although Chester was proud of his role as a "talker," he was also proud of a mural he painted on the side of one of the buildings in Albuquerque as well as his sketches of the animals and Navajo people he grew up with on the reservation. The sights and sounds of the "res" remained dear to his heart. He was always very proud of his Navajo heritage.

Chester Nez died in 2014 at the age of ninety-three. He was the last of the original twenty-nine "talkers" to survive.

The First Navajo Alphabet

(There were additions later)

a: wol-la-chee (ant)

b: na-hash-chid (badger)

c: moasi (cat)

d: be (deer)

e: ah-jah (ear)

f: chuo (fir)

g: ah-tad (girl)

h: tse-gah (hair)

i: tkin (ice)

j: tkele-cho-gi (jackass)

k: jad-ho-loni (kettle)

l: dibeh-yazzie (lamb)

m: tsin-tliti (match)

n: tsah (needle)

o: a-kha (oil)

p: cla-gi-aih (pant)

q: ca-yeilth (quiver)

r: gah (rabbit)

s: dibet (sheep)

t: d-ah (tea)

u: shi-da (uncle)

v: a-keh-di-glini (victor)

w: gloe-ih (weasel)

x: al-na-as-dzoh (cross)

y: tsah-as-zih (yucca)

z: besh-do-tliz (zinc)

Samples of Navajo Words Used in the Code

corps: din-neh-ih (clan)

commanding general: bih-ker-he (war chief)

amphibious: chal (frog)

America: ne-he-mah (our mother)

dive bomber: gini (chicken hawk)

torpedo plane: tas-chizzie (swallow)

observation plane: ne-as-jah (owl)

fighter plane: da-he-tih-hi (hummingbird)

bomber plane: jay-sho (buzzard)

battleship: lo-tso (whale)

aircraft carrier: tsidi-moffa-ye-hi (bird carrier)

submarine: besh-lo (iron fish)

destroyer: ca-lo (shark)

August: be-neen-ta-tso (big harvest)

November: nil-chi-tso (big wind)

December: yas-nil-tes (crusted snow)

artillery: be-al-doh-tso-lani (many big guns)

bomb: a-ye-shi (eggs)

cemetery: jish-cha (among devils)

confidential: na-nil-in (kept secret)

creek: toh-nil-tsanh (very little water)

hospital: a-zey-al-ih (place of medicine)

machine gun: a-knah-as-donih (rapid fire gun)

minute: ah-khay-el-kit-yazzie (little hour)

navy: tal-kah-silago (sea soldier)

plane: tsidi (bird)

pyrotechnic: coh-ha-chanh (fancy fire)

tank: chay-da-gahi (tortoise)

torpedo: lo-be-ca (fish shell)

truck: chido-tso (big auto)

vicinity: na-hos-ah-gih (there about)

village: chah-ho-oh-lhan-ih (many shelter)

Photo Gallery

Four of the original twenty-nine "talkers" who volunteered to become Marines during WW II in the Pacific:

Chester Nez who died in 2014 age 93

Albert Smith who died in 2013 at age 88

Wilfred Billey who died in 2013 at age 90

Keith Little who died in 2012 at age 87

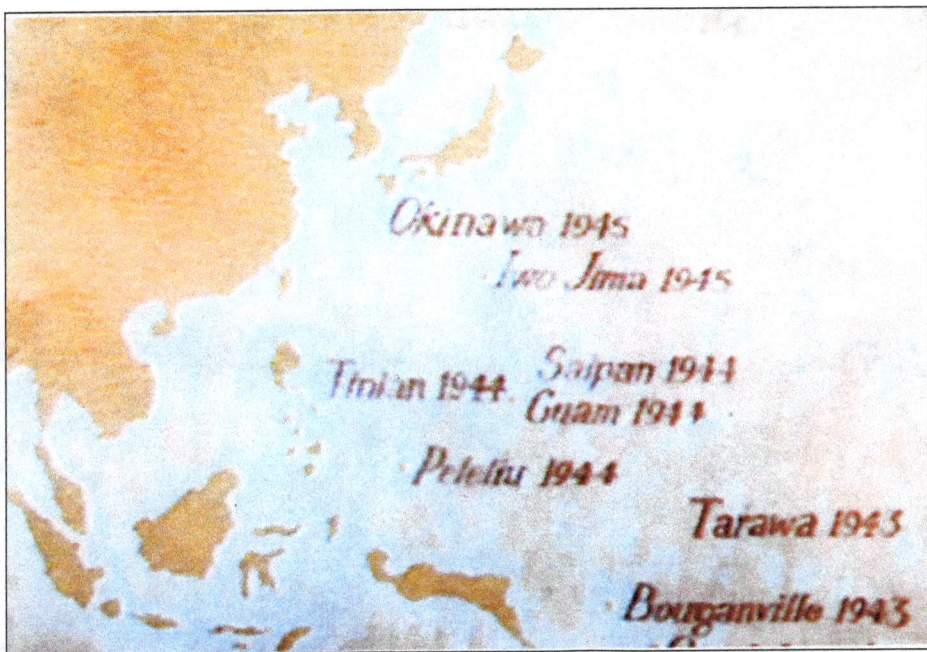

**A map of the Pacific Islands where most of the fighting took place,
courtesy of The Code Talker Museum, Gallup, New Mexico.**

An oil painting by Canku Ota of a "talker" in action accompanied by his white-skinned belegaana companion.

A bronze statue of Wilfred Billey on display at The Gallup Cultural Center in Gallup, New Mexico, created by Orland Joe, sculptor.

Another view of the Wilfred Billey Bronze sculpture created by Orland Joe showing his uniform and the radio equipment.

A large mural on the wall at The Gallup Cultural Center in Gallup, New Mexico painted after the Code Talkers were declassified. The mural was created by Be Sargent.

The Navajo men on Be Sargent's mural are shown making preparations for a Blessing Way ceremony. The Navajo man on the horse wears the traditional turquoise headband and has long jet-black hair.

Another view of the large mural and the Blessing Way ceremony held in honor of the Navajo Code Talkers in celebration of their safe return.

On Be Sargent's large mural at The Gallup Cultural Center in Gallup, New Mexico, the "talkers" are proudly wearing what become the official Code Talker uniform: a red cap, yellow shirt, and turquoise necklace.

Declassifying Heroes

On July 26, 2001, President Bush awarded the Congressional Gold Medal to the original Navajo "Code Talkers" for their success in relaying secret military messages that baffled the Japanese, saved thousands of lives and helped win World War II. Only five of the original 29 Code Talkers are still living. The code was developed after the attack on Pearl Harbor when it was discovered that U.S. military codes had been broken by the Japanese. The overwhelming success of the code caused it to remain classified a full 23 years after the end of World War II. Silver medals were awarded later in the year to the 400 Code Talkers who followed the original 29.

The "Declassifying Heroes" document was created by the Southwest Indian Foundation.

The Code Talkers

It was one of the best kept secrets of World War II. For 23 years, their special mission retained a "top secret" classification. They are the Navajo Code Talkers. The Navajo made an invaluable contribution to the War through the development of the Navajo language as a secret code that proved indecipherable to the enemy. Major Howard M. Connor, communications officer for the Fifth Marine Division commented, "Without the Navajos, the Marines would never have taken Iwo Jima." We salute their remarkable achievement!

The "Code Talkers" document, courtesy of the Southwest Indian Foundation.

Forging a Hero

Early in 2001, we commissioned Navajo artist Oreland Joe to create a larger than life tribute to the Navajo Code Talkers. Oreland Joe was already renowned for other bronze sculptures that he had done around the country. Joe began the work in earnest and in December of that year we unveiled his monumental 8 foot-tall Bronze Code Talker at the Gallup Cultural Center — with many of the surviving Navajo Code Talkers in attendance. You can purchase a limited edition maquette-sized bronze replica of this incredible statue from the Foundation.

"Forging a Hero" document, courtesy of the Southwest Indian Foundation.

www.ingramcontent.com/pod-product-compliance
Lightning Source LLC
Chambersburg PA
CBHW071358090426
42738CB00012B/3158